Love Verses
OF THOUGHT FROM
My Heart

Love Verses of Thought From My Heart

SISTER LEANNA EVANS

XULON PRESS

Xulon Press
555 Winderley Pl, Suite 225
Maitland, FL 32751
407.339.4217
www.xulonpress.com

© 2023 by SISTER LEANNA EVANS

All rights reserved solely by the author. The author guarantees all contents are original and do not infringe upon the legal rights of any other person or work. No part of this book may be reproduced in any form without the permission of the author.

Due to the changing nature of the Internet, if there are any web addresses, links, or URLs included in this manuscript, these may have been altered and may no longer be accessible. The views and opinions shared in this book belong solely to the author and do not necessarily reflect those of the publisher. The publisher therefore disclaims responsibility for the views or opinions expressed within the work.

Unless otherwise indicated, Scripture quotations taken from the King James Version (KJV) – *public domain*.

Paperback ISBN-13: 978-1-66288-414-6
Ebook ISBN-13: 978-1-66288-415-3

INTRODUCTION: This collective of thoughts are not meant to be poems, they are simply how I transferred my thoughts from my heart onto paper and the grammar may seem off, and yet, inside of our own thoughts that only one knows, there can be some certain clear thoughts, mixed with uncertain and not clear thoughts: and one's thoughts can emerge a bit scrambled, but these thoughts, are, our personal truth. It is my prayer that all who read these verses will be inspired to dig deep within oneself and bring out that which is hidden. That, which needs to be expressed. That, which would bring healing to one's heart, mind, body, soul, and spirit.

That, which would reveal the inward person of true self: for one's personal prosperity.

    I have learned by the power of the Holy Spirit, to always keep the love of God in my heart. For this kind of love brings forth blessings in a time of need, power and strength in a time of weariness, and joy, peace, and happiness in a time of lack. Food in a time of famine, and most of all, the substance of faith in a time of hope. In the Holy Bible, **Psalms 4:23 reads: Keep thy heart with all diligence for out of it are the issues of life**. I love this verse, because it let's me know that God is always with me, even when it seems as though He is not. So, I have learned to protect my heart using the breastplate of God's armor, that I may fight the good fight of faith with a sincere heart and to let nothing or no one break it or twist it with anything.

MY HEART ON TODAY: My heart on today is very, very glad because I can feel the love of God within myself; that I have always had. When God created you and me, God did a marvelous thing and no two are alike, except the miracle of identical embryos. My heart on today is very, very glad because all the love God has for me, is the love I have always had, and I love everyone. My heart on today is very, very glad because the love God has for mankind, will always be the same. Love and blessings to you my Holy Father, the one true King; I thank you for my robe and my ring. For the favor of being the daughter of the king, is a privilege and an awesome and wonderful thing.

A GLORY, WITHIN A GLORY: As I set my eyes to look upon God's glory in the sky. I see the clouds all magnificent, rolling and passing by. As I set my eyes to look upon God's glory I think to myself, how I love the vision so, and I wonder how the clouds came to be. When I remember God's glory, I think to myself, this is how God wants the clouds to be.

BROKEN LOVE: When being in love breaks, it can only be that I will love you still. Being in love is always full of hope and promise; making for times to be had. Love in the snapshot pictures that come to be. There are nights of intimacy shared in the privacy of trust, with the plans of staying together forever because thinking and remembering is a must. Then human nature steps in and bends one of the two into a break, and leaves one or two with a broken heart. For when love breaks, it can only be, I love you still. Broken love, means what it means, the two were never meant to be. So, when the two who were broken, learns to forgive the weakness that bends into the break and becomes those tests that are the waters of love; be sure that both wants to fall in love. Because when love breaks and stays broken, it was never true love from the start. So, when I seek to fall in love and to be loved in return, I can only seek a familiar and kindred spirit. Because, still in love, with broken love, is not pretty.

LOVELY: When a seed falls or is planted in good ground, that's where all of the lovely takes place, way down deep and waits for the beauty too spring forth. The eyes wait to behold the moment, when the lovely of the beauty is revealed. Then the lovely of the beauty is forever in the mind of one's heart. Lovely, that which has grown, lovely is that which is within.

FRIENDS ARE ONLY FOR A SEASON: A true friend is not hard to find in the springtime. A true friend is hard to trust at any given time. For a season will come and a season will go, but how the changing of the seasons will come to be, God only knows. In the winter, it can be warm and in the summer, the rain can fall and the sun can shine, both at the same time. Autumn is Fall or is Fall really Autumn: only God can know. Maybe the two are just different spaces of a same season, with inevitable change, but change, nevertheless. Both so pretty with leaves of a wonderful change, an array of bursting, picture painting colors. Then one day into the pretty, the leaves are all gone from the trees and snowflakes and ice crystals is all that we see. For only, God, Jesus, and the Holy Spirit are one all the time and never changing. A friend is only in season, because like a season, a friend decides when the friend inside, comes and goes for whatever reason. Because friends are only for a season, and true, true love is what determines if that friend will be in season forever. Because friends are only for a season. God is true love and God's mercy endures forever, and the seasons of God, are the indicators to endure through one, and be ready to move on to another: because friends are only for a season.

HAVE YOU EVER: Have you ever took the time too watch how the leaves on or off the trees, dance and move to the windy breeze of God's Creation? Have you ever took the time too watch how the grass, and the things upon the grass reacts to the very same breeze? How the breeze does one thing up high, and another thing down low? Have you ever took the time to feel the windy breeze upon yourself, other than too enjoy the calm, cool comfort that a catch in the breeze reveals? Have you ever embraced the notion, that the day breeze and the night breeze are one in the same? Have you ever wondered how the day breeze brings a different sight, than the night breeze, yet, both are the same arrangement of Creation. So now, when one takes in a breeze, day or night, then one is able to say: I have ever.

MAKE ROOM: Sadness is a specific time to rejoice, as it is a time to identify and to overcome the sadness. Knowing that the Holy Spirit loves to hear from us in our prayers, whether sad or glad. For, it is only when we allow the Holy Spirit Father to bring up and purge out our valley sadness, that then, there would be room for His kingdom gladness. So do not be afraid of what makes you sad, tell the Holy Spirit all about it by the silent prayers you pray and by the falling tears rolling down your face, in that secret place. God knows all about each and every tear and God just wants to hear your voice saying, "I will make room." So when

God heals your broken heart of broken spirit, you will know how to accept it. For such sadness, will only be taking up the room, where your joy and contentment should be.

MASTERPIECE: Every day across the sky, God paints a masterpiece. Every day the strokes of His will brings a different vision of a picture, with no day being the same: even as I see the beauty before me, day in and day out. Every day God rolls the clouds in and God rolls the clouds out, creating a fresh and new: Every day Masterpiece for me and you. Why should this masterpiece be important in the eyes of one's spirit of belief? Because God, and not a man, created all that we see. A masterpiece that man can't even touch, although God makes the masterpiece, every day for us. The one and true living God, who, every day, paints a masterpiece, all about, and across the sky.

INSPIRATION: When I attempted to read Maya Angelou's book (*I Know Why the Caged Bird Sings*). I could only read it, just so far. I could only read it, until he disappeared. I could only read it just this far. All my sad memories begin to re-ring; because I can only read the story, just this far. Still I fought to finish the story, but I could not read any further. But the more, and more, I thought about my own molestation; my sadness turned into happy songs. Because now, I am in a whole new time, and a whole new place, that place called forgiveness, just for me. So now, that I am running an adult woman's race, I will be my own personal (*Phenomenal Woman*). Because now I have found my rightful place. I have found my own inward beauty, I have found the me that is no longer molested and ashamed. I have found that broken spirited little girl, and I have grown her up, past the age of twelve. Now, I am sixty years old, and all of me, has caught up together and we make a whole. Yes, I know what it is like to sing sad songs, not being locked in a cage. Yes, I know what it is like to sing songs of joy, being locked in a cage.

I dedicate this (Verse of Thought from My Heart) to Dr. Maya Angelou. May she be resting in the peace that she shared with so many. Thank you for the inspiration of self-expression.

MY BEDROOM WINDOW: I see God in everything, God paints me special pictures in the sky each day, because God has me locked away in the wilderness: the glory prison wilderness God made special, just for me. So now, all I do is look out of my bedroom window. My glory prison is to grow me stronger, and to teach me God's Holy Bible word, my prison of God's glory, is the best thing that has ever happened too me! I see God in the fierce winds of a tornado, and in the eye of a hurricane. I see God in the air that flows, so that mankind can breathe freely as the days go. I can see God when my eyes are open, and I can see God even more, when my eyes are closed. I can feel God in my faith, I can feel God in my heart. I can see God in my heart, when I look at myself in the mirror. I can see God on the pages of my Holy Bible book; and I can see God on the pages of my soul. Have you ever had a front row seat to God's paradise that acts as a prison cell? I have, and I rejoice at the opportunity to be locked away in my glory prison, with God as my warden, and Jesus, the friend who always comforts me in my cell. My bedroom window is a seat that gives me vision, not just sight. My bedroom window allows me to see and hear, all God is teaching me. Through my bedroom window, I can see that place where I am bound. God is in everything; Inside and outside, of my bedroom window.

THE CRASH/THE BURN: When one's living crashes and burns, perhaps one was speeding out of control through the darkness of ignorance, and wickedness of time. For, the crashes and the burns are not always our fault. Because maybe, we just were not taught. The crashes and the burns can most certainly be imposed upon any one of us. Because the wickedness of time works against us, that the judgment of hell might be brought against us. The crashes and the burns effect both, young or old, and the crashes and burns come only because the wickedness of time is filled with dark and bending roads that never seem to end. The crashes and the burns happen when we continue going in circles around the same, exact mountains; crooked and dark, are these. The crash and burn experiences are something mankind does come to know, as mankind continues to grow. The crashes and the burns can be opportunities for triumph and these can be oppressions of being triumphed over. For when the crash and the burn overwhelms us, then we can choose to stay crashed and burned forever: or we can choose to be washed and born again; too also, live forever. So, do not quit at the crashes and burns, because you can win, despite the times one may go through a crash and a burn, a time or two.

WHEN DOES LOVE HURT: Love hurts when you exchange it for worldly purpose. Love hurts when one is happy and the other is sad. Love hurts when love cannot be trusted to do the real and right things. Love hurts when it causes tears of sorrow to fall. Love hurts when you find it in all of the wrong faces and all of the wrong places. Love hurts when you stumble across it by fantasy or by lies. Love hurts when the senses of a predator, is on the prowl to pick up the scent of an innocent. Love hurts when the predator makes a feast of pure lust upon the body parts of other humans. Love hurts when one is blinded by the eyes of sight and when trespasses are made evident by spite. Love hurts between a giver and taker and the bill doesn't get paid, love hurts when it is able to leave you busted, broken, and abandoned and laying at the bottom of a hill. So, what is your love? Do you know which love belongs to you? When does love hurt, when love is stolen by a false heart and taken advantage of by the thief who is hiding behind fake charm and a possessive conversation that lures one into their den, and kicks them over, again and again.

SOMETIMES: Sometimes when you love me, it is really hard to see, but sometimes when you love me I can see the love that you have for me. Sometimes your need to love me, is quite nice, but your want to love me, sometimes throws me a vice. Sometimes you say that I am free to be myself, but if you have the direction in your favor, then sometimes I would be in that glass case, upon your secret mantle. Then sometimes you hide me in your hope chest so that I would not see your best or the best of me, because for real; you never want me to leave.

OUR LOVE: Our love has stood the test of time, and all through the ups and downs, our love still has it's rhyme. Even though our temptations were all over the place and we could not get locked into one another; we stood strong and fast and we did not bail out. So, as a token of my deepest respect, our love has soared way high and above the rest. Now, keep me near, as I will keep you, and our love can continue to do what our love was born to do.

PEARL LOVE: I have been looking all around the world for a soul mate to share my burdens and make me his pearl. So, as I stay here in my very own place, I'm hoping to become the vision that you see, when you investigate your own face. I grow and I grow, only to know someday and in some very special way, that I will be your one and only for sure. So, as I keep my pearl space just for you, I know that the pearls of you and me will continue to know and continue to grow the affections, that will light both our paths home to a place that we built on a mountain of pearls, just for us.

US: When we met that one special day, your heart was in a shell. A shell that covered all your living hell. You fought very hard to keep that shell intact, but the special and unforeseen love you felt for me, was ready to interact. You gave me a real big trinket and some shiny tokens of love: but the realness of your feelings, you did not ever speak of. Now, that we have parted, you say that you want me back. But you and I know that is going to take lots of trust, to make us a true fact: to make us: US.

WINGS: As I spread my wings to fly, I will remember all our days gone by. When you spread your wings to fly, keep me, keep me ever so nigh. As we spread our wings to fly above higher ground forever, there will be our true found love. Way above the earth we will soar, with our wings full. And when we find our resting place, there forever, our love will be at the very best. Nice and sweet, always we will be. Just us, just you, just me in our wings.

THE LOVE: When I look at your world, I can see your whole world. Those big brown eyes are the mirrors that reflect from inside: the inside you simply cannot hide. You told me once, that you loved me, that you loved me deep in your soul. I believed you then, and I believe you now. So let us show each other, every day of our lives, all the honesty and respect and trust and love, that our true hearts of love, cannot ever hide.

ONLY YOU: Only you can make it happen; only you, my sweet cupcakes. Only you came back and made another way. Only you, gave me the final say. Now, my heart belongs only to you; only you for, and only you, it will always be.

AWAY: When you are away from me, my steps are insane. When you are away from me, I cannot complain. When you are away from me, all those necessary hours, I always understand. For, when you are away from me, I think of you only, over, and over again. Because when you are away, it is never very far. But we always stay in tune, that you just must be away sometimes, just driving in your car and listening to, your tunes; thinking that you are away from me too.

LIFE HURTS: I wondered why now, in life, everything seemed to hurt, because it truly did not always hurt. I remember then, and I remember now, I was a sheltered child. Then my living showed up, for the death ride; and it secretly stole my pride. So, life can hurt even more, if you just give up and refuse to live: don't just die. Do not give your life over to the hurt, no way, no how. You must shed that awful hurt. You are more than a conqueror. You came from the dust of God's creation, and you will aways be someone special, someone awesome, someone fearfully and wonderfully made. I had to understand, that it was not life that hurts; but that living hurts.

LET IT FLOW: When I look into your eyes, I see everything and nothing. I see all that you manage to hide. Whenever you dared to express your feelings, thereafter, was always a need for healing. Come now, out of the blue, and follow me to the calmness; of let it flow. Do not cover yourself. Do not be ashamed. Because being true to your own heart, and to the one you love, this will bring you precious, heavenly blessings and fame from above. So, learn to nurture your flow. Your flow will bring you joy and make you remember when it was loving and safe, just to play with your new toys. Now, keep your flow, always abreast, and when your life has ended, you will be led to your peaceful best.

PASSION: As I write the verses of tales, in an ode. My heart, my body, and my soul kicks into overload. I passion out a line or two, then burst of energy grows the sentences of realness, and these touching verses begin to show. Verses that are sprouting from an overdue season. I am so glad that only God, made the raindrops, because God knew, ever so timely, when my love verses of thought, would be sprouting, in their dirt of my due season, and God sent the raindrops for everything to grow out of me. God inspired me to write these verses of tales, each thought, in an ode: in an ode of passions told.

I HAD TO LEARN: There are people I know well; all about me spawning hell. But the stories between us, are not for show and tell. For, to each other, we owe nothing, but unto God, all is due. So, be very careful of who you talk to, and what you say out loud. Because the broods of evil and wickedness awaits all around. Waits around to hear and twist your words, and tangle anything into a jumble of true and false together, that your own story, you cannot recognize or, undo. I had to learn the hard way, that these are always, up to: know, no good. I had to learn, how not to play at the devil's playground. But I once was lost, inside of the devil's playground.

I had to learn that I was capable of really crushing another human being. Honestly, I knew this about myself at a young girl's age. But as I matured, I only crushed the ones who tried to crush me first. Now, I have found my way out of such nightmares and I choose to walk the higher ground. I had to learn.

I WRITE MY FLIGHT: My flight started long before I knew that I was flying. When I finally landed; I realized that I had lived my life, given life, and lived to see more life beyond my own, in my four children and in my grandchildren. Then one day, a fatal infection, threatened to take my life, and I thought I was going to die, before raising my children to their adult size. And for the next twelve years, I avoided the harsh treatments my doctors were recommending, because I could not suffer the thoughts of dying and leaving my children without their own mother. I write my flight, and I did too. I got on my knees to God, and He answered my prayers. I stayed strong and healthy. God allowed me to raise my children. I write my flight, and I did too. My children aged out of the home, and they were good, and so was I. I choose to write my flight, I chose life, not death. My flight is my flight, and today, I still write my flight.

AS I GOT LOST AT THE CROSSROADS: My destination had already been preset. I had already answered the calling of my name from the heavens, out loud. I had always longed for the anointing and all the favor of God's open arms. So, just as I crossed the split in the road with my feet in the air, bam, the darkened shadows of this world, blocked my feet from landing there. The blockage was so high and wide, it blinded my way and my feet fell so very far away, from the place I was suppose to land. I fainted at the crossroads, so exhausted and so weary, a traveler, on fire for love: as I got lost at the crossroads. Then I remembered, I had not read my Holy Bible yet, and I did not have the full wisdom and the complete knowledge, of the power and glory of the crossroads. God had called my new name, out loud, out from the highest of the highest; and, although I was ready in my soul: my heart, my mind, my body, and my spirit were not ready. I had alerted the enemy to my own presence, because I was not prepared, I was not carrying the map of instructions, to endure getting lost at the crossroads; and the darkened shadows hindered me for many years, and kept me from landing at the crossroads. As I got lost at the crossroads. I could not touch down into freedom, the enemy had me blocked. As I got lost at the crossroads. Now, praise be to the omnipresent one, who brought me to the remembrance of faith and renewed my destiny, and set forth an opened space, the narrow way, through the darkened shadows. Then my present showed up, my blessing came forth, and I was able to place both feet firmly on the solid rock of spiritual awareness. As I got lost at the crossroads, I spent that time reading my Holy Bible, and one day, after I had completed my reading and studying, suddenly, the dark shadows were gone, and nothing or no one barred my way. I remember being lost at the crossroads, but now I am forever found at the crossroads.

ADDICTION: Addictions are so hard to break, and one can be addicted to any person, place, or thing. So, do not feed that addiction anymore. Kick that addiction off, and onto the floor. Then stomp it down until it lives no more; not a stick or a seed, not even a glass pipe, feed. Quit now, right now, I know that is easier said than done, because I once had an addiction to the plant of a seed, and one fine day, my addiction tried to kill me, because the poison rose to the top, that's when I gathered all my strength, and I stopped. I stopped getting high because my life force was getting low; lower than it ever had before. I felt myself dying, right there, down on my knees and vomiting like a sick dog. I began having flashbacks of lust and wasted money, and my heart began talking to me and the voice of God, entered in and offered me a brand new start, a brand new beginning. So, stop letting that addiction have control over your flesh, right here, right now. I know, you tell yourself, every time, before you get high, that this is the last time, but guess what, your spirit may be willing, but your flesh is too weak to make the decision. Your flesh will get high, until you die: but through it all, your spirit wants to live. If you need help to quit, then get the help and quit, so that you can stop dying by one's flesh, and start living by one's inward spirit. Understanding that you must refill that space you have emptied out by quitting that addiction. Change your surroundings, get different friends, go to church, meet new people, move if you have too. But please, stop dying, and begin again, and live. The choice is yours.

LOVE YOURSELF: Learn to always love yourself, it is easy, if you try. Practice every day, and the results will find the way. Practice every day, practice every way to always love yourself, it is easy when you try. Love yourself all the time, even when you feel no love from others: no ways, no how's. It is easy, if, and when, you try. The time, money, and effort that you spend on others, spend all that on yourself for a change. For, the change will show up in the mirror, when the person you love, is looking back at you: and never forget, that God himself, lives on the inside of you too. God's kingdom lives within you. So, stop looking around, and look at yourself. True love is a gift, and that's what you are: gifted just to you, from way beyond the stars. So, present yourself to you, every day and in every way, and be the first in your line, to receive the best of your love. Always love yourself first, because you only get one you. Always practice loving yourself: it is easy, whenever, you decide to do so.

TIME: My time is very precious. I did not know this before. So now, as I sit and remember my time that has gone by before. I often think of royal dreams, and precious memories, that now fill my time, thoughts, and streams. Time is not my friend, and yet, because of God's forgiveness, time allows me do overs, now and again. Time keeps me hoping, each day, that when my time comes, to truly die. I will fly away softly, light, and without sin, to hinder my way.

I KNOW: I know, in the heart and soul of my being. There has always been a writer, just waiting to burst out of her dreams. Her work is like no other, because her influence has been, her own personal need to be a loner. With only the company of her Holy Bible, that she took the time to reveal, because her wounded heart and broken spirit, needed special and personal attention too heal. The healing attention, that only God could give. I know her writings are true and very real, and very focused: because they came from the creative scenes, from her own life story. I know, now, that my one true relationship is with God. Why? Because I know what I know: that I know.

SO WHAT: I can stand the pain now, it does not hurt so much anymore. It only throws me straightway to God; the one I truly love, trust, and adore. So, go ahead and pacify me, and think that you are winning. I realize now, that it was a good thing, that you taught me how to do and be without you, from the beginning. So yes, and so what, so what, and so what again. Because I let you know, much too, much too soon, that I loved you since the beginning. So now, so what, you don't want me anymore, that's a good thing for me, because down deep inside of me, I always knew, that you were no good for me. So what, I allowed my flesh to get the best of me, concerning you. Now it is good that I don't have to love you anymore, now, so what.

MY MIRROR: When I look in my mirror, I can see my age. When I look in my mirror, every day is a whole new stage. When I look in my mirror, I smile at myself with wonder. Because when I look in my mirror, my reflection does not reveal all that I've been through. So, when I look into the mirror, just to see. I'm really looking in my mirror, looking just at me. I love me and so does my mirror, because every day, we have something to change, something to make better; and something to never do again.

LONELY: I'm lonely, so lonely, my fake name is Lonely: and oh, so lonely I am. I cannot seem to shake this empty-handed feeling, that is from deep inside of me. Sometimes I feel so all alone, and this does make me cry. Sometimes I feel so all alone, till I just sit, sit, and sit until the time comes, and then goes goodbye. I don't know, just when I fell off my life raft, but I surely know, this moving river of lonely time, is very hard to swim. I plan to help myself, really. I plan to get out one day and find my sailing ship; so back to life, I can go. Back so I can live again, even if It's just only me.

OBVIOUS: When love is obvious, love is always obvious. And the grace of obvious is faithfulness, truth, trust, honesty, protection, respect, and consideration of oneself. Which is in equal, to the obvious missing rib. Love is last and always first, the obvious circle of life, that should be filled with obvious truth. Not the lies of the threatening evil, that can frighten an obvious love, to be a curse. So, in the fullness of undisputed truth, the two should be a collective to the obvious needs and obvious wants. Be ever so committed for the better and for the worst. Be obvious about your love for one another, no matter what. Don't make small talk, and beat around the bush, go straight for the heart and make obvious, the art.

WHEN WE MET: When our eyes met, the stage of our lives was immediately set. Knowing that we would always be together, we sheltered our love, inside, out of the weather. So, as we stand here facing what seems a lifetime ago, there is plenty to be thankful for. From our first hello and our treasured years tossed about, this way and that. There was never any talk of letting go. Now, all the years have gone by, and we both are still very beautiful inside. The hello that we shared the day we met, will be our hello, always and forever. That's how and when we met.

VERSES: Whenever I am creating and then writing down on paper, my love verses of thought, I often tremble inside and out. It comes from the love, and all the special and wonderful things about you, about me, about everybody, I have ever known, both good and bad. Whenever I am creating the unique words, that all come floating outward from within, my bones get shy and my heart wants to tell everything. My verses are true, my verses are deep, and whenever I am writing the verses down. They fall like stars from the sky-to my heart-to my mind-to my soul-to my spirit: and then they all get a home with me, on my paper, forever to be and all to see.

JOY AND HAPPINESS: Joy and happiness are not the same. And their functions and results do vary significantly from one another. Joy stays in the mind, body, heart, soul, and spirit; no matter what breaks.

Happiness comes and goes with every break, and every fix. Because happiness comes and goes, never knowing, when to stay, or to go. Joy stays all the time. Happiness doesn't know if it should be happy or sad. Joy and happiness are not the same, nor compared, nor envious of each other. Joy always chooses to stay, and happiness depends upon the day.

DEPRESSION: Depression can be invisible, and yet, the effects of depression can be very visible. Depression is a thief, a liar, and a cheat. Depression can render one weak and hinder one's own strength. Depression will tell you that nothing is really wrong. And at the same time, tell you that everything is wrong. Yes, depression can be invisible, because depression is a toxin. A build up of residue, left over from the horrible people, places, and things of this world. So, guess what: you are not crazy. Every thing a person thinks, feels, and entertains, is real to that individual. The toxins of depression has the ability, to set itself up in the brain and block the full strength of logic, reason, and clarity. Depression can rob a sound mind, and cause a type of brokenness within the heart and one's spirit. So, do not be tricked, if you have experienced an overload of toxic people, places, and things; the results can be, the depression of a sort. So please, get some help, because your life depends on you. (Smiley Faces).

WORTHY: If you have accomplished the steady job, the dependable car, and that yearly lease or home ownership; then is someone who has any less than these; worthy of you? What do you bring to the table, and what are you expecting to be brought to your table? Are you willing to share what you deem worthy, or, are you willing to be less, in order to feel worthy? Will you settle for less, or will you require equal or more? Who is truly worthy? Most importantly, you must be worthy within yourself first: before giving oneself away to the possibility of worthy. In this world, money answers all things. But, on the inside of yourself, you are worth more than money, worth more than anything.

DO YOU SEE ME: Do you see the real me, or do you see the me that you want to see? Chemistry, is not the true indicator of seeing the me, or the real you. Chemistry can be the fleshly indicator of attraction and reaction. Chemistry is sexy and tricky. Do you see the real me, or do you see the me that you want to see? Chemistry is not the primary, but communication is. Can I see the real you, can you see the real me? Who really knows? So, let's have a real and true conversation and reveal the real me, and the real you.

KALEIDOSCOPE: The kaleidoscope is pretty, but it is all mixed up, and kaleidoscope is my official word for dating. Dating can be a disaster for some, and an absolute thrill for others, regardless of one's sexual preferences. When we meet new people, with dating in mind, we are literally blind to their nature inside. A nature in which, a person governs the affairs of their life. Let's face it, relationships can be one of three types: good, bad, or really nothing. That's just my opinion. Kaleidoscope, pretty, but all mixed up. Looking at all of what you are not familiar with, can be deceiving when it concerns dating. Even if we meet someone via our familiar friends, this is not a guarantee, that a person is sane, and reasonable, and an overall good person. So, be very careful when you decide to date, don't make small talk, go for the jugular and watch them sweat. Discuss the real stuff, ask those embarrassing questions, take advantage of the newness, and pay for your own dinner. Because shelling out money for someone who is a stranger, is not a good icebreaker. Dating is a kaleidoscope, so don't be fooled by all the pretty mixed together colors. Do not be so eager to taste the rainbow. And if sex is all you seek, tell the truth, because that is what responsible adults do.

THE END

www.ingramcontent.com/pod-product-compliance
Lightning Source LLC
LaVergne TN
LVHW021745060526
838200LV00052B/3476